CHRIS KLEIN

Pickleball In No Time

Pickleball Made Simple: A Fast-Track Beginner's Guide

First published by Independently published 2023

Copyright © 2023 by Chris Klein

All rights reserved. No part of this publication may be reproduced, stored or transmitted in any form or by any means, electronic, mechanical, photocopying, recording, scanning, or otherwise without written permission from the publisher. It is illegal to copy this book, post it to a website, or distribute it by any other means without permission.

Chris Klein has no responsibility for the persistence or accuracy of URLs for external or third-party Internet Websites referred to in this publication and does not guarantee that any content on such Websites is, or will remain, accurate or appropriate.

Designations used by companies to distinguish their products are often claimed as trademarks. All brand names and product names used in this book and on its cover are trade names, service marks, trademarks and registered trademarks of their respective owners. The publishers and the book are not associated with any product or vendor mentioned in this book. None of the companies referenced within the book have endorsed the book.

Cover Photo by Chris Klein - Sawyer Point, Cincinnati

First edition

ISBN: 979-8-9891650-0-1

Advisor: Coach Jaime Klein

This book was professionally typeset on Reedsy.
Find out more at reedsy.com

To all those who show fortitude and resilience to achieve their goals.

Just maybe, the go-go-go guy was on to something.

                                                Chris Klein

Contents

Foreword   v

I Let's Start with Something Fun

1. 25 Fun Facts About Pickleball   3

II Introduction to Pickleball

2. Timeline of the Growth of Pickleball   9
3. Origin of Pickleball   12
4. Overview of the Game   13
5. Why Pickleball has Grown in Popularity   15

III QUICK-HIT TIPS

6. Coach Chris Quick-Hit Tips   21

IV Pickleball Basics

7. Court Dimensions and Layout   25
8. Scoring   31
9. Basic Rules Summary   34

V Equipment Overview

10	Types of Paddles and their Characteristics	39
11	Balls: Differences and Selection	42
12	Footwear and Attire	48

VI Basic Techniques

13	Grip and Paddle Handling	53
14	Serving and Return of Serve	58
15	Forehand and Backhand Strokes	63
16	Overhead Smashes	71
17	Dinking: The Soft Game	74

VII Advanced Techniques

18	Spin: Slice, Topspin, and Sidespin	79
19	Bonus Shot: The Backhand Flick	82
20	Third-Shot Drop	86
21	Lobs and Defending against Lobs	90
22	Poaching and Court Coverage	93

VIII Strategy and Tactics

23	Doubles Strategy	97
24	Singles Strategy	100
25	Player Positioning	102
26	Shot Selection	104
27	Reading Opponents and Anticipating Shots	106

IX Fitness and Conditioning

28	Importance of Warm-Up and Cool-Down	111
29	Exercises Specifically for Pickleball Players	113
30	Injury Prevention and Recovery	115
31	Nutrition for Peak Performance	117

X Playing Environment

32	Indoor vs. Outdoor Play	121
33	Weather Considerations	125

XI Community and Social Aspects

34	Finding Places to Play and Local Leagues	129
35	Building a Pickleball Community	132
36	Tournaments and Competitive Play	134

XII Drills and Practice Routines

37	Drills for Improving Specific Skills	139
38	Structuring a Productive Practice Session	141
39	Solo Drills	143

XIII Advancing Your Game

40	Seeking Coaching and Instruction	147
41	Advanced Strategies and Techniques	149
42	Continuing Education and Staying Updated on Rule Changes	153

XIV The Future of Pickleball

43	Evolution of the Sport	157
44	How to be an Ambassador for the Game	159

XV Reasons to Love the Game

45	100 Reasons People Really Like Pickleball	163

46	Conclusion	169
	About the Author	172

Foreword

I've always been drawn to sports, particularly racket sports. From the ping pong table in the basement of our suburban Ohio home, to my travels around Arizona and New Mexico for racquetball tournaments, I've cherished the physical challenges, strategy, and camaraderie that accompany these games.

Unsurprisingly, tennis became my passion in my 30s and 40s. It provided the perfect work/life balance I sought, and after long days at the office, the tennis courts beckoned, ensuring I got the workout I both needed and immensely enjoyed.

These tennis sessions were often followed by social hours with teammates and opponents alike. My love for tennis led me to captain United States Tennis Association (USTA) teams, organize club socials, and travel the globe to play in exotic locations like Austria, Monte-Carlo, Newport, and even Vail. Tennis was, undeniably, a driving force in my life.

The summer of 2018, however, brought a major shift in perspective. While searching for tennis courts in Cortez, Colorado, my wife Jaime and I stumbled upon six bustling pickleball courts. Despite our unfamiliarity with the game, the crowd's enthusiasm was contagious. When we inquired about tennis courts, the response was surprising: "Don't bother looking, but hey, grab a paddle and join us." Though it wasn't exactly love at first dink, the community's spirit, diversity, and togetherness left a lasting impression.

That unexpected day marked the beginning of my deep dive into pickleball. I found that it encompassed all the joys of tennis—cardio, strategy, socialization—but added its own perks and eliminated many of tennis's complications. Pickleball, it turns out, doesn't demand an even-numbered foursome or a pre-booked set of courts, and it welcomes players of all ages and abilities into competitive matches. Simply put, with basic knowledge, anyone can show up at a park or a gym, rack up their paddle, and start playing.

This book will show you how to play pickleball and give you the confidence to immediately get started with the game. Drawing from my years of tennis and pickleball teaching experience, I'll guide you through the key insights I've gained while giving you a broad perspective of the game. You'll learn the rules, comprehend the strategies, get acquainted with the equipment, discover playing locations, understand the fitness benefits, and learn techniques to begin and enhance your game.

So, let's give it a shot. As we discovered in Cortez, Colorado, this game is truly for everyone, and just like that, you too will be playing Pickleball In No Time!

I

Let's Start with Something Fun

Whether you are new to the sport, or an accomplished player, odds are that you don't know all of these facts!

1

25 Fun Facts About Pickleball

Pickleball is a sport that combines elements of tennis, badminton, and ping pong. Here are 25 fun facts about pickleball:

1. **Where It All Started**: Pickleball was invented in 1965 on Bainbridge Island, near Seattle, Washington.

2. **Name Origins**: Despite myths, the game was not named after a dog. It's believed the name comes from "pickle boat," a term in rowing.

3. **First Paddle**: The first pickleball paddle was made of plywood.

4. **Growth**: The sport has seen rapid growth, initially among senior communities, and now among families, due to its ease of participation and simplicity of the rules.

5. **Growth Rate**: Over 36 million people now play pickleball, and since 2019 the sport saw an over 160% increase in participation, making it the fastest growing sport in the U.S.

6. **Official Court Size**: A pickleball court is 20 x 44 feet, and you can fit two to three pickleball courts into one tennis court.

7. **Serve**: Players must serve underhand, striking the ball below waist level.

8. **No Volley Zone (Kitchen)**: The area 7 feet from the net on both sides is the no volley zone, often referred to as "the kitchen." Players cannot volley (hit the ball before it bounces) within this zone.

9. **Double Bounce Rule**: Each side must play their first shot off the bounce, meaning the ball should bounce once on each side before volleys can occur.

10. **Scoring**: Points can only be scored by the serving side.

11. **Game Points**: Standard games are played to 11 points, and players must win by 2.

12. **Paddle Material**: Paddles can be made from wood, aluminum, graphite, and composite materials.

13. **Inclusion**: The sport is played by all age groups and skill levels.

14. **International**: Though it originated in the U.S., pickleball is now played in more than 60 countries worldwide.

15. **Hall of Fame**: The Pickleball Hall of Fame was established in 2017.

16. **Tournaments**: National tournaments now have large cash prizes for winners.

17. **Community Building**: Many communities have built exclusive pickleball courts due to its rising popularity.

18. **Dink Shot**: A soft shot that is aimed to land in the opponent's no volley zone is called a "dink."

19. **Celebrity Players**: Many celebrities, including former professional athletes, have taken up pickleball.

20. **Pickleball Month**: April was declared National Pickleball Month in the U.S. in 2018.

21. **Pickleball Channel**: A digital-only channel dedicated to pickleball offers news, tips, and stories from the world of pickleball.

22. **Adaptive Pickleball**: The game has been adapted for players with disabilities.

23. **Youth Movement**: Though popular among seniors, there's a growing movement to introduce pickleball to younger generations.

24. **Fastest Shot**: The fastest recorded pickleball shot is over 60 mph!

25. **Travel**: Pickleball-themed cruises and vacations have become popular among enthusiasts.

Pickleball is an ever-growing sport with an intriguing mix of history, culture, and athleticism. It's easy to see why so many people have become passionate about it!

II

Introduction to Pickleball

Imagine tennis, badminton, and ping pong all blended into one super sport. That's pickleball! The game with the funny name is taking the recreational sports world by storm, and it shows no signs of slowing down. Pickleball is a racket sport played with a wiffle ball and paddles that are larger than ping pong paddles but smaller than tennis rackets.

2

Timeline of the Growth of Pickleball

1965: Birth of Pickleball

Pickleball was invented on Bainbridge Island, Washington, by three fathers – Joel Pritchard, Bill Bell, and Barney McCallum. The sport was created to provide a fun, accessible game for their families.

1972: Formal Rules & Organization

The USA Pickleball Association (USAPA) was formed to keep up with the rapidly growing sport. The association established official rules and promoted the sport.

1976: First Tournament

The first official pickleball tournament took place in Tukwila, Washington. This event drew players and showcased the competitive nature of the sport.

1984: Trademark & Growth

The name "Pickleball" was trademarked, and Barney McCallum started manufacturing commercial pickleball paddles. The sport began to spread beyond the Pacific Northwest.

2000s: Surge in Popularity

The 2000s marked a significant surge in pickleball's popularity. The number of places to play in the US went from a few hundred to thousands.

2008: International Play

The sport began to gain traction internationally, with countries like Canada, India, and several European nations hosting pickleball events and forming national organizations.

2010: Revised Rules

A revised and updated version of the official tournament rulebook was published, incorporating feedback from the growing pickleball community.

2015: National & International Championships

The USAPA National Championships had over 800 participants, and international events started attracting global players.

2016-2020: Rapid Expansion

Pickleball saw exponential growth in the number of courts,

players, and organizations. The number of places to play pickleball in the U.S. jumped from 2,000 in 2010 to over 8,000 by 2020.

2018: Younger Generations Join In

Traditionally seen as a sport for retirees, the appeal of pickleball began spreading to younger generations. Universities and high schools started incorporating it into their physical education programs.

2020: Pickleball During the Pandemic

Amidst the COVID-19 pandemic, outdoor sports like pickleball gained further popularity. With its requirement for less physical contact than many other sports, it was a safe and social choice for many.

2021 and Beyond: Continued Global Growth

With the establishment of more professional circuits, significant sponsorships, and increased television coverage, pickleball continued to establish itself as a major sport not just in the U.S., but around the world.

3

Origin of Pickleball

Pickleball has its roots in the summer of 1965 on Bainbridge Island, Washington. Joel Pritchard, a U.S. Congressman at the time, Bill Bell, a successful businessman, and Barney McCallum, a friend, are credited with creating the sport. The story goes that after returning home from a game of golf, the trio discovered their families were bored with the usual summertime activities. In a stroke of creativity, they set up a badminton court. However, they couldn't find a shuttlecock. Instead, they improvised with a wiffle ball, lowered the net, and fabricated paddles from plywood.

The name "pickleball" has an amusing origin. While some believe the name derived from the Pritchards' family dog, Pickles, who had a penchant for chasing stray balls, Joan Pritchard, Joel's wife, clarified that the name came from the term "pickle boat", which refers to the last boat to come in during a rowing race.

4

Overview of the Game

Pickleball is a hybrid racket sport that fuses elements of tennis, badminton, and table tennis. The game is typically played on a rectangular court, significantly smaller than a tennis court, which is bisected by a net. Doubles or singles play is possible, with participants using solid paddles to rally a specialized, perforated plastic ball across the net.

The serve in pickleball is executed underhand, originating from below the waist. It must be directed diagonally into the opponent's service box. Following the serve, the receiving team must let the ball bounce once before returning it, adhering to the "Double Bounce Rule," which mandates that the ball must bounce once on each side before volleys or other gameplay is allowed.

Another intriguing aspect of pickleball is the existence of the "No Volley Zone," nicknamed "the kitchen." This is a seven-foot space on either side of the net where players are not allowed to volley the ball; instead, they must allow it to bounce once before executing a return.

The scoring system operates on a rally-scoring basis, but uniquely, only the serving team has the opportunity to score points. The game culminates when one team reaches at least 11 points with a minimum lead of two. Therefore, if the score reaches a 10-10 tie, the game continues until one team establishes a two-point lead.

As for equipment, pickleball players use paddles that are more rigid than those used in either badminton or tennis. These can be made from various materials, including wood and composite substances, providing a sturdy and responsive hitting surface. The ball used in pickleball is also distinct; its perforated, wiffle-like design allows for optimal aerodynamics, but its robust construction ensures durability.

In summary, pickleball offers an engaging and strategic gameplay experience, characterized by unique rules such as the Double Bounce Rule and the No Volley Zone. These features, along with its inclusive nature, make pickleball a captivating sport suitable for enthusiasts of all ages. Whether you're an active participant or an avid spectator, the multi-faceted appeal of pickleball is bound to capture your interest.

5

Why Pickleball has Grown in Popularity

In recent years, Pickleball, a seemingly unexpected sport, has been making waves, gathering fans from all age groups and backgrounds. While the name might elicit a chuckle or two, the game's popularity is nothing to laugh at. Let's delve deeper into what makes pickleball the fastest growing sport in the country.

The first thing to understand about pickleball is its accessibility. The beauty and draw of pickleball lies in how straightforward it is. With its uncomplicated rules, beginners can dive right in and soon find themselves engrossed in the game. When I teach, it is my goal to have the beginners playing out real pickleball points within the first hour of instruction. And almost without exception, they are playing out points at the 30-minute mark, and playing real games for the last 20 minutes of the hour.

Another notable aspect of pickleball is the physical demands it places – or rather, doesn't place – on players. Tennis, its more recognized counterpart, can be rigorous, often straining the knees and elbows. In contrast, pickleball offers a gentle approach, making it especially attractive to older players. Yet, its appeal isn't limited to any age group. "The rules and equipment were designed to blur the lines between age and gender," pro Irina Tereschenko said in a recent Forbes article about pickleball inclusivity.

From kids to grandparents, pickleball courts are filled with diverse players. And as the game attracts younger players, the playing pace and cardio workout accelerate even further.

What really makes Pickleball awesome, however, are the social dynamics of the game. Pickleball stands out as a highly social sport due to its inclusive nature, straightforward rules, and community-centered ethos. Its accessibility draws individuals from diverse age groups and skill levels, fostering a rich environment for interaction and camaraderie. The relatively relaxed pace of the game allows for conversation and socializing, both during and between matches. Moreover, the sport's structure, often featuring doubles play, naturally promotes teamwork and communication. Local courts serve as community hubs where friendships are formed and strengthened, and organized leagues, tournaments, and social events amplify this sense of community. All these factors coalesce to make pickleball a unique social experience, far beyond just a physical contest.

On the practical side, pickleball scores high in affordability. Unlike some sports that require hefty investments in equipment or venues, pickleball remains relatively inexpensive. Whether it's setting up a new court or getting the basic gear, costs are manageable, opening doors for more enthusiasts to join in.

The game's versatility also stands out. No need to worry about the weather ruining your plans; pickleball adapts. While a sunny day is perfect for an outdoor match, indoor courts ensure that rain or cold doesn't put a damper on the fun. This adaptability extends to existing sports facilities too. Across towns, former tennis, badminton, and basketball courts are finding new life as pickleball venues.

Driving the sport's popularity from behind the scenes are organizations like the USA Pickleball Association (USAPA), Pickleball Canada Organization (PCO) and the International Federation of Pickleball (IFP). These groups tirelessly champion the sport, standardizing rules, promoting events, and fostering a nationwide community of pickleball aficionados.

Lastly, the embrace of the wider community cannot be overlooked. Across neighborhoods and cities, local governments and community leaders have recognized pickleball's charm. New courts pop up in parks, tournaments draw in crowds, and community centers offer indoor pickleball classes.

In essence, the rise of pickleball is a testament to its inclusive nature, its ease of play, and the sheer joy it brings to participants. It serves as a reminder that sometimes, the most straightforward pastimes can create the most significant impact. Whether you're a seasoned sports enthusiast or a curious newcomer, pickleball beckons with a promise of fun and friendship.

III

QUICK-HIT TIPS

In individual or small-group lessons, I generally find that players new to the game pick it up very quickly, and most can be playing out full points within the first hour of play. Here are my favorite quick-hit tips to help you start playing Pickleball In No Time!

6

Coach Chris Quick-Hit Tips

- **Serve Deep** - Hit your serve high and deep. The returner will be challenged to wait for the bounce, and won't be able to take the return while moving to the no volley zone.
- **Return Deep** - Put air under the return of serve. High and deep will keep your opponent back while you get to the no volley zone line.
- **Get to the Line** - Following the serve and return, all four players should be working to get up to the no volley zone line, and once there, to stay at the line.
- **Hold the Line** - You get to the line, now hold the line! Take small steps to handle shots, and try not to get moved back from the no volley zone.
- **Dink Defensively** - Keep your dinks low and unattackable, and let your opponent's make the error.
- **Drops, Not Drives** - Focus on more 3rd shot drops and less drives. Drives are easy to block and defend, while drops will lure your opponent into unforced errors.
- **Paddle Up** - The key to being ready for the next shot is

to always bring your paddle back to the "Ready Position". Having your paddle up and in front of your body will enable quick responses to the next ball.

- **Take the Ball at its Apex** - When hitting a ball after it bounces, don't let it drop. Take it at its highest point.
- **Keep Your Elbows Tucked** - The main reason shots go flying in an unintended direction is that your body positioning gets "loose." With your paddle up and in the ready position, your elbows will be tucked and your shots be more consistent.
- **Watch the Opposing Players Paddle** - To know where the next ball will go, keep an eye on our opponent's paddle. The direction of their paddle will likely show you the direction of their shot.
- **Bungee Cord with Your Partner** - You and your doubles partner should move in sync, shifting left to right and forward and backward. Imagine being on a bungee cord with your partner to enhance your court coverage.
- **Shoulder High, Let it Fly** - If the ball is coming at you high or fast, let it go past, as it will likely land out of bounds.
- **Upgrade Your Equipment** - Getting started playing pickleball is inexpensive, but as your game accelerates so too should your equipment. A mid-range paddle that has a carbon fiber surface and a honeycomb interior will improve your game and soften the impact on your joints.

IV

Pickleball Basics

Now that we know about pickleballs origins, and why it has become the fastest growing sport in the country, let's take a look at the basics of the court layout, the scoring and the rules.

7

Court Dimensions and Layout

The Court

The easiest way to visualize the pickleball court is to call it a mini-tennis court, but as we delve into the specifics, you'll discover the nuances that distinguish pickleball courts from their tennis counterparts. With precise lines and a small yet easy-to-move court, a pickleball court is designed for the sport's mix of skill, power, and accuracy.

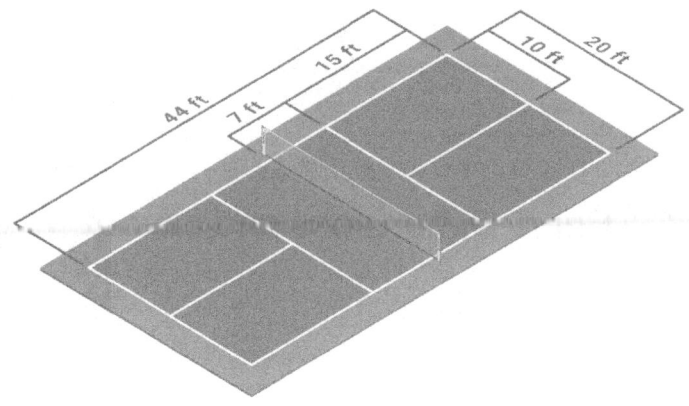

Pickleball Court

The Divider: The Net

The dimensions of a pickleball net are similar to those of a tennis net, but slightly shorter. A standard pickleball net is 36 inches (91.44 cm) tall at the sidelines and 34 inches (86.36 cm) tall at the center. This lower height accommodates the sport's dynamic gameplay and allows players to engage in exciting rallies over the net. The net is placed in the middle of the court, spanning the width, and is a crucial element in shaping the strategy and flow of pickleball matches.

Where to Serve: The Service Areas

Every game has its rules, and in pickleball, you need to serve

COURT DIMENSIONS AND LAYOUT

the ball from a particular spot and aim it to land in a specific area. The court has sections called service areas or boxes. Each side of the net has two of these boxes, one to the left and one to the right. They're quite spacious, being 15 feet long and 10 feet wide. So, when you're serving, these are your target zones!

Beginning the Serve

The Special Zone: The No Volley Zone

One of the things that makes pickleball stand out is a unique area called the "no volley zone" or, by its nickname, the "kitchen." This zone covers 7 feet from the net on both sides. It's marked clearly, and it comes with a unique rule: If you're inside this zone, you must wait for the ball to bounce once before you hit it. No smashing allowed here! This rule makes pickleball a game of skill and patience, and it levels the playing field so that players of all ages and skill levels can enjoy competitive games.

Drilling Behind the No Volley Zone

Wrapping Up

The pickleball court, with its unique dimensions and special zones, brings a distinctive flavor to the game. By understanding the court's layout, players can strategize better and enjoy the game even more. The next time you're on or near a pickleball court, you'll see it from a new perspective, appreciating the intricacies that make this sport so enjoyable.

8

Scoring

Like every sport, it's important to know how to keep score when playing Pickleball. But once you learn the basics, you'll find it's not too tricky, and I always tell new players to not worry about the score, because the players around you will gladly advise you!

Every pickleball game begins with a score of 0-0-2. Now, you might be wondering, "Why not start at 0-0-0?" Here's the reason: the first number shows the serving team's score, the second number represents the receiving team's score, and the third number indicates which server is up - the first or the second. This is because in pickleball, **both players on a team get a turn to serve before the ball goes to the opposing team.**

As an example of how it works, let's say that you are the serving team and the score is 7-9-2. This means that your team has 7 points, the opposing team has 9 points, and the second player is serving. If you lose the rally, then the opposing team gets to serve, and the score becomes 9-7-1, meaning that the opposing team has 9 points, your team has 7 points, and the opposing team is on their first server.

Now, here's an important thing to remember: **only the serving team can score points.** If the serving team wins a rally, which means the other team misses the ball or makes an error, they get a point. But if the serving team loses the rally, they don't earn any points. Instead, the next player on their team gets to serve. If they don't manage to score during their turns, then the serve goes to the other team.

When the game starts, the *first serve is made from the right-hand side of the court.* If the team serving scores, then the server moves to the opposite side, which is the left-hand side, for the next serve. They'll keep switching sides every time they score. However, if they don't score, their partner gets a chance to serve from their side.

To win a pickleball game, a team has to score 11 points. But, and this is a big "but," you need to win by at least 2 points. This means if both teams have 10 points each, the game isn't over. The play continues until one team has a 2-point lead, even if that means going well past 11 points.

Sometimes, in special tournaments or more official matches, games might be played up to 15 or even 21 points instead of just 11. So, always be ready for longer games when in competition!

Lastly, there is one more important rule to understand about serving. On the first serve of the game, only one player from the serving team gets a chance to serve. This means that the

SCORING

score at the beginning of a game is called out as 0-0-2. After this, both players on each team get a turn to serve. It's a unique quirk that applies only to the first serve of the game.

Coach Chris Tip: When you are learning the sport, don't focus too much on keeping track of the score. Instead, focus on the most basic aspects of the game, such as consistent serves and returns, and a consistent dinking strategy.

So, while pickleball scoring might seem a bit different at first, with a little practice, it will become second nature. And to be sure, everyone loses track of the score at one point or another, especially in recreational play. If it happens to you, don't fret, you have three other players to help things get back on track!

9

Basic Rules Summary

The following is an abbreviated form of the rules to give a quick overview of how the game is played.

Serving:

- Players must serve underhand, with the paddle's face below the waist and the ball hit below the server's waist.
- The serve is made diagonally to the opponent's service court.
- Only one serve attempt is allowed, except in the event of a "let" (the ball touching the net but still landing in the correct service court).

Double Bounce Rule:

- When the ball is served, the receiving team must let it bounce once before returning. Then, the serving team must also let it bounce once before playing. After these two bounces, the ball can be volleyed (hit without bouncing).

No Volley Zone:

- Players cannot volley (hit the ball before it bounces) while standing in the no volley zone.
- The player cannot step into the zone and volley the ball, even if the ball is outside of the zone.

Scoring:

- Pickleball can be played as singles or doubles.
- Points are scored only by the serving team.
- Games are typically played to 11, win by 2.

Sequence of Play and Rotation:

- In doubles, the serving team has two players serving, starting from the right-hand court. Once the first server loses their serve, their partner serves from the left court. After they lose the serve, the opposing team gains the serve.
- Players rotate sides with their partner after scoring a point when they are the serving team.

V

Equipment Overview

Choosing the right gear not only enhances your performance but also keeps you safe and comfortable on the court. From paddles and balls to court shoes and even portable nets, the options are endless. However, the sheer variety of equipment available can sometimes feel overwhelming rather than empowering.

10

Types of Paddles and their Characteristics

Wood Paddles

In the early days of pickleball, paddles were crafted from wood. These paddles are heavier than most other types. Because of their weight, they can give the ball a powerful hit, but they might also make your arm feel tired faster. On the bright side, they are usually less expensive than other paddles and are known for their durability. However, if you're looking for finesse and control, wooden paddles might not be the first choice.

Graphite Paddles

Fast forward to the present, and you'll find that graphite paddles have become a favorite among many players. These paddles are lightweight, making it easier for players to control the ball and move the paddle with agility. Their surface is strong, allowing players to make powerful shots confidently. Though they are on the pricier side compared to wooden paddles, many players believe the cost is a worthy investment for the gameplay benefits they offer.

Composite Paddles

Composite paddles are an interesting blend of various materials. They can be made from a combination of things like fiberglass, aluminum, and even polymer. Because they come in a mix of materials, you can find them in both heavy and light versions. One standout feature of composite paddles is their textured surface. This texture can help players put a spin on the ball. Price-wise, they typically sit between wood and graphite paddles, making them an option worth considering for many.

Polymer Paddles

Moving on to polymer paddles, these are crafted from a specific type of plastic material. They are generally lightweight, which many players find advantageous for swift movements. Durability is another strong point for polymer paddles; they can handle a lot of action on the court without showing signs of wear. And when it comes to your budget, they strike a balance. They won't set you back as much as a graphite paddle, but they will be more expensive than the wooden variety.

Grip Size and Length

Beyond just the material, players should also consider the grip size and length of the paddle. A grip that feels comfortable in your hand can significantly influence how well you play.

Similarly, the length of the paddle can affect your reach on the court and how you strike the ball. Always try holding a paddle before making a purchase to ensure it's the right fit for you.

Coach Chris Tip: Paddles generally fall into three pricing and quality categories: beginner, intermediate and advanced. For perspective, a beginner paddle might cost about $25, intermediate about $100, and advanced up to $250. Beginner paddles are great to get started with, but don't wait too long to upgrade you paddle and take your game to the next level.

With so many pickleball paddles available, each boasting its unique features, players have abundant choices. Whether you're just starting out or have been playing for years, there's a paddle out there that's perfect for you. It's not just about the price or the material but also about how it complements your gameplay. So, the next time you step onto the court, think about the role your paddle plays in helping you deliver your best performance!

11

Balls: Differences and Selection

Introduction

Imagine stepping onto a court, hearing the soft thud of a paddle hitting a perforated ball, and seeing it soar over a net. That's the charm of pickleball, a game that has fascinated many. But what about that ball? Isn't it just another wiffle ball? Not quite! This chapter will guide you through the maze of pickleball balls and help you choose the best one for your game.

The Ball's Role in the Game

In the world of sports, the type of ball used can dramatically shape the game's flow and pace. This holds especially true for pickleball. The ball you choose can affect your game strategy, the way you hit, and even the game's outcome. So, it's not just about any ball; it's about the right ball.

Indoor vs. Outdoor Balls

BALLS: DIFFERENCES AND SELECTION

The primary distinction in pickleball balls lies in their intended location of play.

<u>Indoor balls</u>, for instance, are designed keeping the calm, controlled environment of an indoor court in mind. They usually have about 26 holes, which are relatively larger. Their lighter weight complements the absence of external elements like wind. Moreover, these balls provide a soft bounce, fitting the smoother surface of indoor courts.

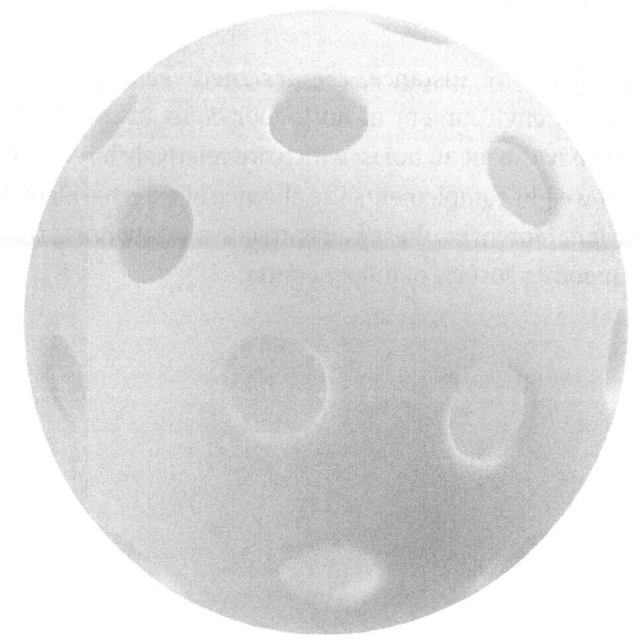

Indoor Ball

On the other hand, <u>outdoor balls</u> are built to combat the challenges of the unpredictable outdoors. With around 40 smaller holes, they are structured to fare well against breezy conditions. They are slightly heavier, ensuring they aren't easily swayed by the wind. Their bounce is consistent, taking the rougher texture of outdoor courts into consideration.

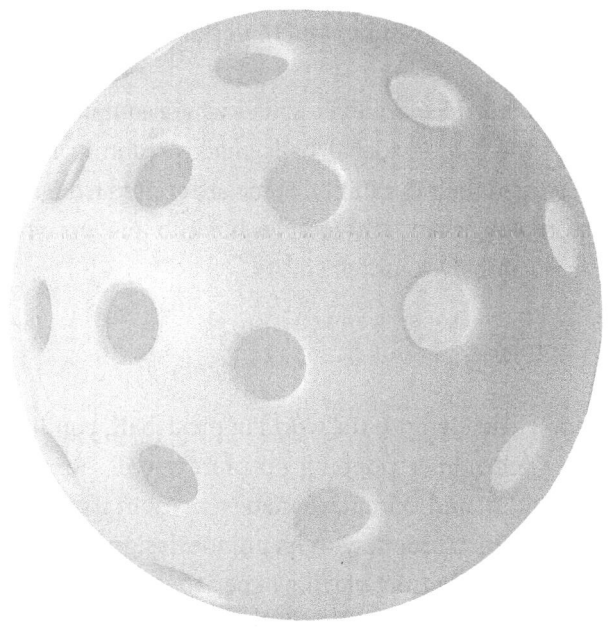

Outdoor Ball

The Significance of Color

While you might initially consider the color of a pickleball ball a mere aesthetic choice, it serves a functional purpose. Bright shades like neon or yellow are often chosen because they starkly contrast with the court, ensuring better visibility for players. So, when picking a ball, it might be wise to select one that stands out distinctly against your playing surface.

The Ball's Build: Durability and Material

Materials matter. Especially in sports where equipment undergoes wear and tear. Pickleball balls, made predominantly from plastic, vary in their durability. Some are crafted from tougher plastics, making them a preferable choice for players who play often or on abrasive outdoor courts.

Brand Influence

As you delve deeper into the world of pickleball, you'll notice certain brand names popping up more often. Brands like Onix, Franklin, and Dura have made a mark in the pickleball ball market. Each brand, with its unique design and material choices, offers a distinct playing experience. It's beneficial to sample balls from multiple brands to ascertain the one that resonates with your playing style.

Tips for Selection

When standing in front of an array of pickleball balls, remember these points. First, be clear about where you'll predominantly be playing – indoors or outdoors. This decision will guide your primary ball type selection. Secondly, don't shy away from experimentation. Sometimes, playing with different balls provides insights into your own preferences. And lastly, lean on the pickleball community. Fellow players can often provide invaluable advice based on their experiences.

Coach Chris Tip: Most of the time, pretty much any standard ball such as the Franklin X-40 will perform just fine. So don't get too hung up about the ball, and instead focus on your strokes and strategy.

12

Footwear and Attire

The Importance of Proper Footwear in Pickleball

There's a lot of movement involved when playing pickleball. Quick dashes, sharp stops, and rapid turns are all part of the game. This is why the shoes you wear play such a vital role. They don't just protect your feet; they can also enhance your performance!

Safety is a primary concern. Imagine trying to run across the court in slippery shoes. Not only would it be difficult, but it could lead to unnecessary slips or falls. Wearing shoes with a good grip helps prevent accidents.

Additionally, when your shoes support your feet correctly, it's easier to focus on the game. Comfort goes hand in hand with performance. If you're distracted by sore feet or shoes that pinch, you can't give your best to the match.

Tips for Choosing Pickleball Shoes

When shopping for pickleball shoes, there are a few things you'll want to look out for:

- **Grip and Traction:** Shoes with a non-slip sole are essential. They help you navigate the court safely, ensuring that your feet have the best grip on the surface.
- **Support:** Court shoes are specifically designed for the rapid lateral movements and quick pivots common in the sport. The lateral support of a tennis shoe is crucial to protect the player from potential injuries and to provide stability during play.
- **Fit:** Just as with any footwear, the fit is crucial. A shoe that's too tight might cause discomfort, while one that's too loose could lead to trips or falls. Always try on pickleball shoes and walk around to ensure a snug fit.

Dressing Right for Pickleball

Beyond shoes, the rest of your attire matters too. Opt for lightweight clothing, preferably made of materials like polyester. These fabrics keep you cool, even as you move around a lot.

When choosing bottoms, go for comfortable shorts or skirts. Some players prefer ones with pockets to stash an extra ball. As for tops, T-shirts or tank tops that allow freedom of movement are best.

If you're playing outdoors, consider wearing a hat or visor. It shields your face from the sun and can also help reduce glare, letting you keep your eye on the ball.

Lastly, don't forget the socks! Socks with cushioning and support can further enhance the comfort provided by your shoes.

Coach Chris Tip: Protect your eyes. The pickleball can't really hurt you, but a direct or inadvertent ball to the eye can do real harm. Wearing protective glasses or goggles is always a good idea.

VI

Basic Techniques

As in any sport, mastering the fundamentals is essential to advancing your game. This chapter will introduce you to the basic techniques that will provide a strong foundation for your pickleball journey.

13

Grip and Paddle Handling

When we talk about the "grip" in pickleball, we're referring to the way you hold the paddle. Just as there's a correct way to hold a pencil for writing, there's a particular way to hold a pickleball paddle.

Imagine you're about to greet a friend. You'd reach out and shake their hand, right? Holding a pickleball paddle is somewhat similar. This type of grip, where you hold the paddle as if you're shaking someone's hand, is called the "Handshake grip" or the "Eastern grip". Your thumb rests at the back of the handle, and your pointer finger is stretched along the side. This grip provides a good balance between power and control, and it is the most versatile grip for a wide range of play.

Handshake Grip

It is essential, however, not to grip your paddle too tightly; a relaxed hold is key. If you clutch the paddle too firmly, it can restrict your swing and reduce your control over the ball. Think of holding a small bird in your hand. You'd want to hold it securely so it wouldn't escape, but not so tight that you might harm it. That's the ideal pressure for your grip!

Another common style is to modify the Handshake grip by running one or two fingers up the backside of the paddle. The advantages of this grip are increased stability, especially for your backhand shots, and it can assist in achieving more power and consistency. The major downside, however, is a reduced hitting area on the backhand side of the paddle.

Two-Finger Grip

Coach Chris Tip: Try the standard Handshake grip first, and then if you need more control try switching to the modified grip with one or two fingers extended onto the paddle.

14

Serving and Return of Serve

You really only need two main skills to get started playing out points, a serve and return of serve, and the ability to dink the ball across the net, which we will discuss in detail later in this section.

Here, we'll dive deep into two moves that set the rhythm of the game: the serve and the return of serve. By mastering these techniques, you're well on your way to becoming a confident player on the courts.

The serve is the grand opening of every point in pickleball. It's the moment one player sends the ball flying to the other side, announcing, "The game is on!" The importance of a good serve cannot be overstated; it sets the tone for the entire point.

When serving in pickleball, the key is to use an underhand motion. Imagine your arm swinging like a pendulum, starting from below your waist and moving upwards. Your paddle should gracefully brush the bottom of the ball, giving it just the right lift and direction. As for your stance, keep one foot firmly planted behind the baseline. It's important not to step on or over this line until the ball is in play. And remember, in pickleball, we always serve diagonally. If you're on the right side of your court, aim for the right side of the opponent's court.

My favorite serve and return of serve is the "**Rainbow**." By serving high and deep (a rainbow) you are keeping the returning player on their heels, making it difficult for them to hit an effective return. And similarly, when you return high and deep (a rainbow), the serving team is forced to wait for the deep return to bounce before they can start moving up to the no volley zone. And while they are stuck waiting, you and your partner are now at the no volley zone line, and holding an advantage over the serving team.

But what happens after the serve? This is where the return of serve comes into play. The ball sails to your side of the court, and it's your moment to respond.

Being ready is half the battle. Stand poised with your knees slightly bent, and your paddle up and in the ready position. Your eyes should be glued to the ball from the moment it leaves your opponent's paddle. As it approaches, take a confident step forward, connecting with the ball after it has made its first bounce on your side. The trick is to aim deep into the opponent's side of the court, making their next move a challenging one.

In pickleball, there's something called the "double bounce rule." This means that after the serve, the ball must bounce once on each side before players can volley or hit it in the air without letting it bounce. It adds a layer of strategy to the game, and this rule, along with the no volley zone rule, are what makes pickleball such an awesome sport. These rules level out the game to make it fair for everyone on the court.

To wrap up, both the serve and the return of serve are foundational to pickleball. While it might take a little while to perfect these moves, remember that practice makes perfect. Keep your eye on the ball, enjoy each game, and soon enough, you'll be serving and returning like a pro.

Coach Chris Tip: Mix up your serves occasionally to keep the opponent guessing. A surprise short serve can sometimes throw off an opponent's rhythm.

Here's to many fun-filled games on the court!

Rules for Serving

- **Underhand Motion:** When you serve in pickleball, you must use an underhand motion. This means your paddle should move from low to high, and your arm should swing from below your waist.
- **Foot Position:** Both feet must stay behind the baseline when serving. Be careful not to step on or over the line before you hit the ball.
- **Serving Diagonally:** The serve must go diagonally across the court. So, if you're on the right side of your court, you should serve to the right side of the opposite court.
- **Land Past the No Volley Zone:** All of the lines in pickleball are considered "in" if the ball lands on them, but the one

SERVING AND RETURN OF SERVE

exception is that the serve must land **past** the no volley zone line, or else it is a fault.

How to Hit a Good Serve

- **Stance:** Stand with your feet shoulder-width apart. This gives you balance.
- **Grip:** Hold the paddle with a "Handshake" or "Eastern" grip.
- **Focus:** Look at where you want the ball to go. Take a deep breath and concentrate.
- **Swing:** Remember, it's an underhand motion! Swing your arm smoothly, brushing the bottom of the ball with your paddle.

The serve is the only shot in pickleball over which you have 100% control, so take advantage of it!

Return of Serve

Once the serve has been made, the ball will come to your side of the court. It's now your job to hit it back.

Tips for a Good Return of Serve

- **Get Ready:** Stand with your knees slightly bent and paddle in front of you, ready to move.
- **Watch the Ball:** Keep your eyes on the ball from the moment it's served.
- **Step Forward:** As the ball comes to you, step forward with

one foot and hit the ball after it bounces once on your side.
- **Aim Deep:** Try to hit the ball deep into the opponent's side of the court. This makes it harder for them to hit it back quickly, and will give you extra time to get up to the no volley zone (kitchen) line, alongside your partner.

In conclusion, serving and returning the serve are crucial in pickleball. With practice, you'll get better and better at these moves. Remember to always keep an eye on the ball and enjoy the game!

Key Takeaways:

- The serve starts the point in pickleball.
- Use an underhand motion and make sure that both feet stay behind the baseline when serving.
- Use the "Rainbow" serve and return of serve strategy to keep your opponents deep in the court.

15

Forehand and Backhand Strokes

As with any sport, mastering the basics is crucial. In pickleball, two essential strokes can enhance your game: the forehand and the backhand.

Understanding Forehand and Backhand

When you think about playing pickleball, picture yourself on the court, paddle in hand, and the ball heading your way. How the ball approaches you will determine whether you will use a forehand or backhand stroke.

The "forehand stroke" is when you swing the paddle from the side of your body that your palm faces. On the other hand, the "backhand stroke" is the opposite. Here, you swing the paddle from the side of your body opposite to where your palm faces.

Perfecting the Forehand Stroke

To begin with the forehand, you first need to have the right grip. Imagine you're about to shake hands with someone. This handshake grip, known as the "Eastern grip," is ideal for pickleball.

Position yourself with feet shoulder-width apart. Make sure your toes are pointing towards the net and keep a slight bend in your knees. This stance helps you be ready for any shot.

Keeping a keen eye on the ball is vital. As it approaches, time your swing. As the ball gets closer, step forward with one foot. Swing the paddle from back to front in a low-to-high motion. It's essential to maintain a smooth swing to get a controlled shot. Once you've hit the ball, continue the swing, allowing the paddle to rise above your shoulder. This action is known as the "follow through" and it helps in giving direction to your shot.

Forehand Stroke

Mastering the Backhand Stroke

For the backhand, you'll use the same "Eastern grip." Your stance remains the same: feet shoulder-width apart, toes towards the net, and knees slightly bent.

When you spot the ball coming towards your backhand side, prepare by turning your shoulders. This slight rotation ensures that the side from which you're hitting faces the net.

Taking a step forward with the foot opposite to the paddle hand, swing the paddle from back to front in a straight line. The swing's direction might feel different from the forehand but remember to keep it smooth. After making contact, let the paddle swing naturally, finishing the motion near the opposite shoulder.

Backhand Stroke

Beginner players often ask if it's acceptable to use a two-handed backhand, similar to the backhand they use in tennis. The answer is yes; it's perfectly acceptable to use a two-handed backhand, and it's relatively common at all levels of play. Just keep in mind that if you choose this technique, you'll want a paddle with a slightly longer handle to accommodate both hands.

Now, imagine holding a paddle in your hand and getting ready to hit the ball. The way you swing the paddle can be either:

- **Forehand:** Swinging the paddle from the side of your body that your palm faces.
- **Backhand:** Swinging the paddle from the side of your body opposite to where your palm faces.

Let's break down how to do each stroke properly.

The Forehand Stroke

Step-by-step guide:

- **Grip the Paddle:** Hold the paddle with an "Eastern grip."
- **Stand Ready:** Stand with your feet shoulder-width apart. Your toes should point towards the net, and your knees should be slightly bent.
- **Watch the Ball:** Keep your eyes on the ball as it comes towards you.
- **Swing the Paddle:** As the ball gets closer, step forward with one foot and swing the paddle from back to front. Your paddle should move in a smooth, low-to-high motion.
- **Follow Through:** After hitting the ball, let your paddle

continue its swing until it is above your shoulder.

The Backhand Stroke

Step-by-step guide:

- **Grip the Paddle:** Keep the same grip as the forehand, the "Eastern grip."
- **Stand Ready:** Just like in the forehand, your feet should be shoulder-width apart with your toes pointing towards the net. Your knees should be a little bent.
- **Watch the Ball:** Always keep your eyes on the ball.
- **Turn Your Shoulders:** When you see the ball coming to your backhand side, turn your shoulders so the side you're hitting from is facing the net.
- **Swing the Paddle:** Step forward with the foot opposite to the paddle hand and swing the paddle from back to front. This time, swing it in a straight line.
- **Follow Through:** Let your paddle continue its swing, but this time, it should end up near the opposite shoulder.

Practice, Practice, Practice!

Both forehand and backhand strokes can initially seem challenging, but consistent practice will make them second nature. A few key things to always remember: always keep an eye on the ball, stay mobile, and keep practicing. Engaging in fun matches with friends or family can make this learning process even more enjoyable.

Coach Chris Tips to Remember:

- Always watch the ball.
- Keep your feet moving.
- Practice both strokes often.
- Play with friends or family to make it more fun!

16

Overhead Smashes

You're on a pickleball court and the ball is lobbed high in the air towards you. Instead of just tapping it back, you raise your paddle up high, wait for the ball to come close, and *WHAM!*—you hit it down hard into the opponent's side of the court. That powerful hit is called an overhead smash.

Using an overhead smash at the right time can be a game-changer. Here's when you might want to use it:

- **When the ball is high in the air**: It's easier to hit a powerful smash when the ball is above your head.
- **When you're close to the net**: Being near the net means you can hit the ball down at a sharp angle, making it hard for your opponent to return.
- **When your opponents are out of position**: If your opponents are too far back or too close to the net, a smash can catch them off guard.

Here's how to hit the overhead smash:

- **Get Ready**: As soon as you see the ball coming high toward you, get into position. Stand with your feet shoulder-width apart, facing the net.
- **Track the ball**: Keep your eye on the ball. This helps you time your smash perfectly.
- **Swing with power**: As the ball approaches, swing your paddle from behind your head, hitting the ball at the highest point you can reach.
- **Follow through**: After hitting the ball, let your paddle continue its motion. This helps ensure a strong and controlled smash. There is a lot going on here, so most importantly, make sure you hit the ball inbounds.

Once you have the basics down, here's how to improve the stroke:

- **Practice, Practice, Practice**: The more you practice, the better you'll get. Start by having a friend toss the ball to you so you can practice your smash.
- **Watch and Learn**: Watch experienced players. Notice how they move, where they stand, and how they swing. Try to mimic their moves.
- **Stay Calm**: Sometimes, you might miss or hit the ball out of bounds. That's okay! Keep calm and try again.

Coach Chris Tip: The key to an effective overhead smash is to watch the ball closely with your hitting hand up high in the air, but also to have your non-hitting hand up in the air to track the incoming flight of the ball. Here's how that shot looks:

OVERHEAD SMASHES

Overhead Smash

17

Dinking: The Soft Game

When watching a pickleball game, you might have seen players gently tap the ball back and forth over the net, almost like they're having a calm conversation with their paddles. This soft tapping game has a special name: "dinking."

Dinking is the most important shot to master in pickleball. If you can master this simple-looking shot, you will put yourself in a position to win points by causing your opponents to make unforced errors.

Here's how it's done:

Dinking is the act of softly hitting the ball. Instead of giving it a strong whack, you just give it a gentle push—just enough to send it over the net but not too far into the opponent's court. It's like playing a delicate game of catch with your opponent, where the aim is not to throw hard but to keep the ball low over the net and going back and forth. Your grip on the paddle should be loose, while keeping your wrist stiff. Remember, the key to

DINKING: THE SOFT GAME

effective dinking is that it is a defensive shot, intended to create an error by your opponent that allows you to win the point.

Dinking is important because it gives players a fantastic level of control over the game. When you're dinking, you get to decide exactly where the ball should land, making it really tricky for your opponents to predict or hit back. It's also a brilliant strategy move. Sometimes, opponents prepare themselves for a hard hit. But when they see a soft dink coming their way, they might get surprised and make a mistake.

To master the dink shot in pickleball, envision you're softly tapping a delicate object. That's exactly how your touch should be on the ball. Gentle and controlled. Also, it's important to bend your knees and keep your paddle low. This stance helps you better guide the ball. And don't forget to keep your eyes glued to the ball. By doing so, you can quickly decide where it should go next. But remember, dinking isn't about being the fastest; it's about being patient. Wait for the right moment, watch your opponent's move, and then decide how to play your shot.

One occasion to use the dink shot is when you're up against a player who has a reputation for smashing the ball. These types of players are called "**Bangers**," and dinking can throw them off balance. As players improve their games, Bangers tend to win less points than Dinkers, so use this as motivation to continually improve your dinking game.

When you're playing doubles, dinking can be a way to communicate with your teammate, setting them up for a smashing return. And if you find yourself close to the net, a dink can be your best bet. It's safer than hitting the ball hard and potentially making an error.

Lastly, as with anything new, practice is key. The more you dink, the better you'll become at it. Grab a friend and spend some time gently hitting the ball back and forth. Challenge yourselves to a dinking duel and see how long you can keep it up without errors!

So, while dinking might look simple, it's a strategy-packed move in pickleball. It's not always about power; sometimes, a soft touch can win you the game. So, the next time you step onto the pickleball court, remember the key strategy of dinking. It can be the ace up your sleeve and win you points by causing your opponents to make unforced errors.

Coach Chris Tip: Practice dinking cross-court and down-the-line until you can reliably place the ball where you want it.

VII

Advanced Techniques

Welcome to an in-depth journey into some of the most critical, yet often misunderstood, aspects of pickleball. Whether you're a newcomer eager to learn or a seasoned player aiming for that next level, this chapter will serve as your comprehensive guide to mastering four key areas: Spin (Slice, Topspin, and Sidespin), Third-Shot Drops, Lobs and Defending against Lobs, and Poaching and Court Coverage.

18

Spin: Slice, Topspin, and Sidespin

Now let's take a deep dive into the exciting world of spin and some smart strategies to level up your game.

Spin: Slice, Topspin, and Sidespin

Have you ever watched the ball swerve, curve, or bounce differently because of the way it was hit? That's because of spin! Here's a breakdown of three common types of spins:

- **Slice**: This is when you hit the ball so that it spins backward. A sliced shot can make the ball skid or stay low, making it tricky for the opponent.
- **Topspin**: Imagine brushing the top of the ball when you hit it. This makes the ball spin forward. It often drops faster and bounces higher.
- **Sidespin**: Hit the ball from its side, and it'll spin sideways. It can make the ball curve left or right in the air.

Coach Chris Tip: Experiment with spins during practice. You'll soon discover how they can be a secret weapon in your games!

Third-shot Drop

Pickleball has a unique rule. After the serve, both sides need to let the ball bounce once before volleying (hitting without letting it bounce). The third shot is usually the server's partner's shot, and **it's super important!**

Instead of driving the ball, try a "third-shot drop." This is a soft shot that gently arcs over the net and drops into the no volley zone. It's a great way to set up your team for success!

Coach Chris Tip: Practice this shot until you can drop it close to the net, making it hard for the opponents to hit a strong return.

Lobs and Defending Against Lobs

Lob: A lob is a high shot that sails over your opponent's head, pushing them back to the baseline.

- *When to use it:* Use the lob when you notice your opponents are close to the net, or to give yourself time to reset.

Defending Against Lobs: Someone lobbed against you. You got this! Here's how to handle it:

- Move quickly towards the baseline.
- If you can't hit it before it bounces, let it bounce once and then return.
- Try to hit a strong shot, aiming deep in the opponent's

court.

Coach Chris Tip: Practice running backward to defend against lobs, so you're always ready when one comes your way.

Poaching and Court Coverage

Poaching: In pickleball, poaching is when you cross into your partner's side to hit the ball, especially when you think you have a better shot.

- *When to do it*: Poach when you're confident you can surprise the opponents or make a better shot than your partner.

Court Coverage: This is all about moving around and covering as much of the court as possible.

- Always communicate with your partner.
- Make sure you and your partner move together as a team.
- Keep an eye on where the ball is and where your opponents are.

Coach Chris Tip: Trust your partner and always talk to each other. A good partnership can cover the court effectively!

With these techniques and strategies in hand, you're now ready to up your pickleball game! Remember, practice makes perfect. So, grab your paddle and see you on the court! In our next chapter, we'll explore even more advanced techniques to further hone your skills.

19

Bonus Shot: The Backhand Flick

The Backhand Flick in pickleball is a swift, sharp stroke that allows a player to quickly redirect or increase the pace of the ball, typically when near the net or when receiving a low ball.

It is executed using the backhand side of the paddle, with the player snapping their wrist forward and upward, generating a sudden burst of speed on the ball. Unlike the traditional sustained follow-through seen in many other shots, the backhand flick has a shorter, more abrupt finish.

This shot is particularly useful for surprising opponents during fast-paced net exchanges, or when looking to place the ball aggressively into open spaces. Mastery of the backhand flick can provide players with a versatile tool to counterattack or maintain an offensive edge during play.

BONUS SHOT: THE BACKHAND FLICK

Flick Start

Flick Middle

Flick Finish

20

Third-Shot Drop

One of the most pivotal shots in pickleball, the third-shot drop, serves as the bridge between defense and offense. A well-executed third-shot drop can neutralize the advantage held by your opponents at the net and allow you to transition forward. This chapter aims to provide an in-depth understanding of the third-shot drop strategy, from the fundamentals to advanced tips.

One of my favorite rules in Pickleball is the two-bounce rule. After the serve, both sides need to let the ball bounce once before volleying (hitting without letting it bounce). The third shot is usually the server's partner's shot, and it's super important!

Instead of driving the ball, try a "third-shot drop." This is a soft shot that gently arcs over the net and drops into the no volley zone. It's a great way to set up your team for success!

The third-shot drop is more than just another stroke in the pickleball playbook; it's a tactical maneuver that serves as

THIRD-SHOT DROP

a cornerstone for building a strong offensive and defensive strategy. This chapter will delve deep into this crucial play, from its mechanics to its role in the overall game strategy.

At its core, the third-shot drop is a soft, arching shot aimed to land gently in the opponent's no volley zone, commonly referred to as the "kitchen." The ideal third-shot drop is a delicate balance of precision and timing, designed to force the opponent to lift the ball, relinquishing their dominant position at the net.

The third-shot drop serves several strategic purposes:

- **Neutralizes the Opponent's Position**: Your opponents are likely positioned at the net, giving them an advantageous volley position. A well-executed third-shot drop makes it difficult for them to attack your return.
- **Transition to Offense**: A successful third-shot drop allows you and your partner to advance to the net, setting up a more offensive position.
- **Reducing Errors**: By opting for a soft shot, you minimize the risk associated with more aggressive options, like the drive, which can easily go out of bounds or into the net.

The effectiveness of the third-shot drop is dependent on its execution, and mastering the basics is crucial. For starters, grip matters a lot. A handshake or eastern forehand grip provides the necessary wrist flexibility and control required to execute this shot effectively.

- **Stance:** Stand with knees slightly bent, weight on the balls of your feet, and be ready to move in any direction.
- **Paddle Preparation:** have the paddle out in front and ready to meet the ball.
- **Contact Point:** The contact point should be out in front of your body. This gives you the control needed to execute a soft shot.
- **Follow-Through:** This is crucial for control and direction.

Reading your opponents and shot selection are crucial aspects of executing a successful third-shot drop.

Reading Your Opponents

- **Body Language**: Look for cues in your opponents' positioning and body language. Are they leaning forward, expecting a drive? Are they backing off, expecting a drop?
- **Paddle Position**: A high paddle position often indicates readiness for a volley. A lower paddle might suggest preparation for a groundstroke.

Shot Selection

- **Cross-Court or Straight**: Aiming the shot diagonally across the court often gives you more margin for error. However, if an opponent is weaker on one side, a straight shot might be more effective.
- **Depth**: Aim to drop the ball as close to the no volley zone line as possible without risking a fault. This forces the opponents to make a difficult decision on whether to volley

or let it drop.

As you grow more comfortable with the basic third-shot drop, you can begin to incorporate advanced strategies into your game. For example, changing the pace or spin on the ball can add an element of surprise. An occasional fast-paced drive as your third shot can also be effective. This not only keeps your opponents on their toes but also makes your subsequent drop shots more unpredictable and therefore more effective.

Being prepared for the follow-up shot is also crucial. The third-shot drop is not an end in itself; it's a setup for the next series of plays, which could include a volley, dink, or another strategic shot.

The third-shot drop is an integral part of a successful pickleball strategy. Its mastery requires attention to both physical technique and strategic understanding of the game. When executed correctly, it can neutralize your opponents, create offensive opportunities, and elevate your overall game. Understanding its mechanics, importance, and nuances is key to becoming not just a good pickleball player, but a great one.

Coach Chris Tip: Practice this shot until you can drop it close to the net, making it hard for the opponents to hit a strong return.

21

Lobs and Defending against Lobs

Now, let's talk about the strategic shot called the **lob**. You hit the ball high, making it sail over your opponents, and pushing them towards the baseline. This can be a great play when you see your opponent's crowding the net. But what if you're on the receiving end of a lob? The key is to move back swiftly. If you can't get to the ball before it bounces, let it take one bounce and then send a strong return deep into the opponent's court.

- *When to use it*: Use the lob when you notice your opponents are close to the net, or to give yourself time to reset.

Defending Against Lobs: You've been lobbed! Here's how to handle it:

- Move quickly toward the baseline, but be careful running backward, as this can lead to injuries from a fall.
- If you can't hit it before it bounces, let it bounce once and then return.
- Try to hit a strong shot, aiming deep in the opponent's

court.

Coach Chris Tip: Practice running backwards to defend against lobs, so you're always ready when one comes your way!

Defending Against the Smash: An opponent smashes a ball back when you're deep in the court. Here's how to handle it:

- Block, don't swing.
- Stay low and bend your knees.
- Stay relaxed and rely on your reflexes

Defending the Smash

22

Poaching and Court Coverage

Another exciting strategy to consider is **poaching**. Poaching is about seizing opportunities! Sometimes, during a game, you might feel that crossing over to your partner's side to hit the ball will give your team an advantage. This is called poaching. It's a bold move, and it can catch your opponents off guard. However, always be careful when doing this, as it could leave a part of your court exposed.

- **Here's the key to making it work:** Poach when you're confident you can surprise the opponents or make a better shot than your partner.

Always keep in mind, however, the importance of **court coverage**. Pickleball is a game of movement and positioning. It's essential to work in tandem with your partner. Communicate, keep an eye on the ball, and make sure you're covering the court effectively.

For example, let's say that you are on the forehand side and you see a medium-speed ball traveling cross-court towards your partner. To communicate effectively, you should call out "mine!", and your partner should take a step back and prepare to cover your side of the court. Similarly, if you call "yours!" then your partner will know that you are staying put, and that they are clear to take the ball without risking a collision.

Coach Chris Tip: Trust your partner and always talk to each other. A good partnership can cover the court effectively!

VIII

Strategy and Tactics

Pickleball is a thrilling game, filled with swift movements and exciting challenges. Whether you're out on the court with a partner in doubles or facing an opponent solo in singles, a strong strategy can make a significant difference in how you play. Let's delve into the many tactics you can employ to give yourself the edge.

23

Doubles Strategy

Playing doubles means you and your partner are a team, working together to outsmart the opponents on the other side of the net.

One of the most crucial elements in doubles play is communication. Always maintain a dialogue with your partner during the game. A timely shout of "mine" or "yours" can ensure both of you aren't going for the same ball or, worse, leaving it for the other.

In doubles, each player has a side of the court to cover. Ensure you stick to your side and guard it fiercely. This way, you both reduce the chances of any balls whizzing past you unchecked.

Interestingly, one of the most effective strategies in doubles is to *aim your shots down the middle of the court*. This creates confusion for your opponents. They might hesitate, each thinking the other will take the shot, and that split-second delay can be all you need to score a point.

- **Communication is Key!** Always talk to your partner. Let them know if you're taking a shot or if they should take it. A simple "mine" or "yours" can make a big difference.
- **Cover Your Side**: Stay in your lane. Make sure to cover your half of the court so that no balls pass you on your side.
- **The Middle is Gold**: Aim your shots down the middle of the court. This can confuse your opponents and make it hard for them to decide who will hit the ball.

Doubles Strategies – What to Think About

- **Teamwork**: Communication with your partner is key.
- **Positioning**: One person up, one person back? Or both up at the net? Decide as a team.
- **Shared Responsibility**: You and your partner can share serving and defending.

Remember, your partner is your TICKET to winning the game. They're not holding you back — they're not sabotaging your game. They're giving their 100%! Keep the energy positive and your partner will feed off of it. If you're negative, they'll absorb it as well and lower any and all chances of winning the match.

Coach Chris Tip: Have verbal cues like "yours," "mine," or "switch," which means to switch places with your partner to optimize your court coverage.

Doubles Strategy – At the Line and in the Ready Position

24

Singles Strategy

Singles is a different ball game altogether. Here, you're your team. The entire court is yours to defend and dominate. But, compared to doubles, it is also seldomly played, so it probably will not be your main focus.

Being alert is the name of the game in singles. Without a partner to rely on, you need to be ready to dart to any part of the court at a moment's notice. The rhythm of the game is also in your hands. Depending on your opponent's strengths and weaknesses, you might decide to slow the game down or speed it up, disrupting their flow.

- **Stay Alert**: Without a partner, you have to cover the whole court. Be ready to move fast!
- **Control the Pace**: Sometimes, slowing the game down or speeding it up can throw off your opponent. Don't be afraid to change things up.

Singles Strategies - What to Think About

SINGLES STRATEGY

- Speed and Stamina: You'll need to move quickly.
- Skill Shots: More chances to use slices, spins, and drop shots.
- Self-Reliance: You make all the decisions; no need to worry about a partner.

In terms of the rule's differences between doubles and singles, there really aren't any, except that only one player serves until they lose a point.

Both singles and doubles pickleball have their merits. Singles is great if you like to control the game and get a solid workout. Doubles is awesome for socializing and teamwork.

Coach Chris Tip: Varying the height and pace of your serves can keep your opponent off balance and allow you time to get to the no volley zone line quickly!

25

Player Positioning

No matter the mode you're playing, positioning on the court is paramount. When serving, always initiate from behind the baseline. Once you've served, your goal should be to approach the net and set your positioning at the no volley zone line. Dominating the net region gives you an advantageous position, allowing you to respond aggressively to returns and making it challenging for your opponent to score.

Remember, a good pickleball stance means keeping your feet apart and knees slightly bent. It ensures agility, allowing you to make those quick dashes when needed.

- **Serve High and Deep**: Always start your serve from behind the baseline, and get the ball to land deep on your opponent's side.
- **Move to the Net**: After serving, try to get to the net, even if it takes two or three shots to get there. This is where you can take control of the game and make it harder for your

PLAYER POSITIONING

opponent to score.
- **Stay Balanced**: Keep your feet apart and your knees slightly bent. This will help you move quickly in any direction.

Coach Chris Tip: When playing doubles, you and your partner should be on a six-foot bungee cord, moving in sync with each other.

26

Shot Selection

The shots you choose can define the match. Sometimes a well-timed lob, a shot that arcs high over your opponent's head, can push them back, disrupting their position. At other times, a soft, strategic drop shot that lands close to the net can force your opponent to scramble forward.

Of course, there's always the option to power through with a drive—a fast, low shot that can catch your opponent off guard.

Choosing the right shot at the right time can win you the point!

- **Use the Lob**: This is a high shot that goes over your opponent's head, pushing them back.
- **Try the Drop Shot**: This is a soft shot that lands close to the net, making your opponent rush forward, and potentially creating an opponent error.
- **Drive it Hard**: A fast, low shot can surprise your opponent and give you the advantage.

SHOT SELECTION

Coach Chris Tip: Watch your opponents and their movement to decide which shot is best in the moment. If they are staying back in the court, hit a third-shot drop; If they are moving forward, drive the ball to cause them to hit while moving, which is a key way to create an errant shot.

27

Reading Opponents and Anticipating Shots

The game isn't just physical; it's mental too. Pay close attention to your opponent. The angle of their paddle can often give away the direction of their shot. Sometimes, their eyes or the positioning of their feet can provide hints about their next move.

And don't forget to learn from the match as it progresses. If you notice patterns or repetitive shots, anticipate them and plan your countermove.

- **Watch Their Paddle**: You can often guess where the ball will go by looking at the angle of your opponent's paddle. Follow their paddle to see where the shot is likely to go.
- **Look at Their Eyes and Feet**: Often, players look where they're going to hit. Their feet can also show which direction they might move.
- **Remember Past Points**: If your opponent keeps making

the same shot over and over, be ready for it and surprise them with a different response.

Coach Chris Tip: In life and in sports, people go with what they know. If they hit a shot and it works, expect to see it again and again until you show that you are prepared for it. And when they go to their backup shot you will have an advantage!

IX

Fitness and Conditioning

Pickleball is a fun and exciting game that people of all ages love to play. But like all sports, it's essential to stay in shape and keep our bodies ready for the game. This chapter will teach you about the importance of getting ready before a game, some exercises to help you play better, how to avoid injuries, and what foods to eat to play your best.

28

Importance of Warm-Up and Cool-Down

Our muscles are fascinating. Imagine a rubber band. If you've ever tried to stretch a cold rubber band, you know it doesn't stretch well and might even snap. But if it's been gently warmed up, it stretches with ease. Our muscles behave similarly.

Before jumping straight into a game of pickleball, it's vital to warm up. This means doing a series of light exercises to get your blood pumping and prepare your muscles for action. Not only does this improve performance, but it also decreases the chance of injury.

After a spirited game, it's tempting to collapse onto a bench and rest. But just a few minutes of cooling down can make a big difference. Stretching and gradually bringing your heart rate down can help in muscle recovery and ensures you won't feel overly stiff the next day.

Coach Chris Tip: Warm up by doing a short series of drills that will help you get loose and also help improve your skill and technique. Start with some dinking back and forth to your partner, then have one person move gradually back in the court until they reach the baseline, then moving quickly back to the no volley zone. Repeat for each partner, and practice dinking, third-shot drops, and driving the ball.

29

Exercises Specifically for Pickleball Players

The unique movements in pickleball, from swift lateral motions to powerful serves, require strength in specific muscle groups.

One great exercise is the lunge. It strengthens your legs and improves balance, which is essential for those rapid changes in direction on the court. To do a lunge, step forward with one foot and lower your body until both knees form a right angle. Then, stand back up and repeat with the other foot.

Arm swings are another beneficial exercise. They're fantastic for your shoulders and can enhance your serving and volleying power. Simply stand up straight and swing both arms in gentle circles.

Lastly, the sideways shuffle. This move imitates the side-to-side motion you often do on the court. Start with your feet apart and quickly shuffle a few steps to one side and then back.

Coach Chris Tip: Don't forget to stretch your Achilles tendons! The quick-burst running nature of pickleball will put a lot of strain on them, so being limbered up is key.

30

Injury Prevention and Recovery

Safety First!

Injury prevention should be a primary focus from the minute you step on the court. No pickleball match is worth the price of getting hurt, so keep these tips in mind.

Wear the right shoes. Proper pickleball or tennis shoes offer a grip tailored for court surfaces, providing lateral stability and helping to ensure that you don't slip during an intense rally.

And always remember to listen to your body; if something doesn't feel right, or if there's pain, it's a signal to stop and rest. Overexerting can lead to serious injuries. In the unfortunate event of an injury, allow your body ample time to recover. Rest, ice if needed, and consult with a medical professional if the pain persists.

Coach Chris Tip: When teaching beginners, I advise them to keep it simple and follow this strategy: Serve Deep, Return

Deep, Get to the no volley zone Line, and HOLD the no volley zone line. Running backwards from the line to chase a ball is a bad idea when you are learning the sport, and it can lead to falls and other injuries. If you <u>hold</u> the Line, you will find that most shots either come to you or fly long out of bounds!

31

Nutrition for Peak Performance

What we eat can affect how we play. Think of your body as a car. A car needs the right fuel to run its best. Our bodies are the same!

Hydration is the key. Our muscles need water to function optimally. So, always ensure you're drinking enough water before, during, and after your games.

The food on your plate matters too. Proteins, found in foods like chicken, fish, and tofu, are the building blocks for our muscles. Carbohydrates, like rice, bread, and pasta, provide the energy needed to keep going. And of course, fruits and veggies are packed with essential vitamins and minerals, ensuring overall well-being.

When it comes to the mental side of the game, if you've recently tried pickleball, you're probably doing your brain-health a favor. Not only does the sport help with hand-eye coordination and proprioceptive function but it also doubles as a social activity—and we likely don't have to remind you how crucial social bonding is for longevity.

Coach Chris Tip: Always throw a protein bar in your bag. You never know when you are going to need a pick-me-up!

X

Playing Environment

Have you ever wondered where the best place to play pickleball is? Or how different settings might affect your game? This chapter is all about understanding the world of pickleball playing environments and how to play your best game no matter the surface or conditions.

32

Indoor vs. Outdoor Play

Depending on where you live, the season of the year, and the current weather conditions, you may have options for either indoor or outdoor play.

Indoor environments offer a consistency that's hard to beat. The lighting remains the same throughout your game, ensuring the sun won't obstruct your vision. Furthermore, without the wind, the ball's trajectory remains predictable, allowing you to focus solely on your opponent's moves.

However, there's another side to the coin. Playing pickleball outside, perhaps in a park, a backyard, or a local club, brings a different kind of excitement. The feeling of the sun on your back, the fresh air, and the natural surroundings can elevate the experience of the game.

But the outdoors also brings challenges like dealing with the sun directly in your eyes, or the wind influencing the ball's path. Yet, for many, this unpredictability is what makes the game more challenging and exhilarating.

How to Show Up and Play at an Outdoor Public Court

Let's say that once you have read the book and hit some practice balls, you want to go to a local park and play. Here's how you do it:

- Check that there's a specified "open play" time. This way you do not need to show up with anyone, but if you do, that's OK too.
- There should be a rack with paddles in it, known as "racking up," that allows players to place their paddles next in the line to play.
- Players will come off of their court when the game ends, and two or four new players will take the court.
- When your paddle comes up, tell whomever you are set to play with that you are a Newbie. Typically, they will welcome you and explain further how the player rotations on the courts operate at that location.

Adapting to Different Court Surfaces

The surface you play on can greatly influence your game. Indoor courts, for example, are often made of wood like those you'd find in a gym. These courts are generally smooth and can sometimes feel a bit slippery. This is why wearing shoes with a good grip is essential when playing indoors.

On the other hand, outdoor courts have their own unique characteristics. They can be made from materials like concrete, asphalt, or even specialized sport tiles. These surfaces might occasionally have small cracks, or they might become slippery when it's just rained.

The key to mastering different courts is **practice**. The more you play on a particular surface, the more intuitive it becomes to predict how the ball will bounce or how quickly you should move.

Weather Considerations

Weather is a major factor to consider, especially if you're playing outdoors. On bright, sunny days, the sun can sometimes make it challenging to spot the ball. Wearing a hat or sunglasses can be beneficial in these conditions.

Windy days offer a different kind of challenge. The ball might not always go in the direction you expect it to, adding an element of surprise to every play. It's crucial on such days to stay alert and be flexible in your movements.

Rain, while it might seem fun, can be tricky. Wet courts are notorious for being slippery, and it's best to wait for them to dry before playing to ensure everyone's safety.

Lastly, always consider the temperature. On hot days, keep yourself hydrated, and during colder times, ensure you're dressed warmly enough but still comfortable to move.

In wrapping up, where and how you play pickleball can shape your experience of the game. Whether you're battling it out indoors or embracing the challenges of the great outdoors, being aware of your surroundings and preparing accordingly can ensure every game is a memorable one.

Coach Chris Tip: When playing outdoors, it's good idea to switch sides of the court when the score gets to six. That way the effects of the wind and the sun are fair for both teams.

33

Weather Considerations

The weather can be a big game-changer, especially when playing outdoors.

- **Sun**: On bright sunny days, it might be harder to see the ball, especially during midday. A cap or sunglasses can help.
- **Wind**: A windy day can make the ball move in unexpected ways. It can be a challenge, but also fun. Remember to watch the ball closely and be ready to move!
- **Rain**: Wet courts can be slippery. If it's raining, it's best to wait until the court is dry. Safety first!
- **Temperature**: In very hot weather, make sure to drink lots of water. In cold weather, wear layers so you can stay warm but also move easily.

Coach Chris Tip: Always be prepared! Knowing what the weather is going to be like can help you get ready for your game.

XI

Community and Social Aspects

Community is what makes pickleball so special. And as communities around the country have listened and responded to requests for more pickleball courts and open play times, the ability to play at any time of the day or night has become a reality. That leads us to the first step to playing pickleball, by finding out where the action is happening.

34

Finding Places to Play and Local Leagues

The first step to diving into pickleball is figuring out where the action is. Many local parks have set up pickleball courts due to its rising popularity. When you visit, you might even find schedules posted for times when players gather to play.

If you're not sure where to start, then start with the internet. A simple search for "pickleball courts near me" can lead you to a nearby spot. In addition to parks, many community centers now have indoor courts where you can play year-round, no matter the weather outside, and these community centers often cater to beginner players.

For those who want a more structured experience, joining a local league can be a fantastic option. These leagues often host regular meetings for players to engage in friendly matches. They cater to a variety of skill levels, from beginners just starting out to experienced players wanting to improve their game.

Here is the path that I follow when looking for places to play.

- **Search Online:** Websites and apps are available that list pickleball courts by location. Type "pickleball courts near me" into your search engine.
- **Visit Local Park District Locations and their Websites:** Many local parks now have pickleball courts, and some have schedules posted for when people usually play. I start by going to the website of the local park district, and typing in "Pickleball." Places, times, and even skill levels that are welcome will be displayed.
- **Local Community Centers and the YMCA:** Many community centers have indoor courts where you can play, and the YMCA's, JCC's, churches, and other facilities with gyms have begun to bring in new people by setting up pickleball courts. And why not? We've clearly established that pickleball is the perfect social sport for all ages and abilities.
- **Local Pickleball Clubs:** The future of recreational pickleball will be a combination of public indoor and outdoor spaces and private clubs. All across the country, new venues have sprung up, with grand openings happening on a weekly basis. While more expensive than public courts, they offer the convenience of a weather-free environment along with the ability to make reservations and to meet new like-minded friends.
- **Join a Local League:** This is a group of players who meet regularly to play. Leagues can be for fun for learning, or for competition. Ask around or search online to find one near you!

Coach Chris Tip: My favorite website for locating courts when I travel is Pickleheads, www.pickleheads.com. Their search results will show you both private and public spaces, number of courts, and if they are lighted for nighttime play.

35

Building a Pickleball Community

Playing pickleball is an exhilarating experience, but the fun multiplies when shared with friends. If you've discovered the joy of the game, why not invite a friend or family member the next time you head to the court? They might find themselves just as enamored with the game as you are.

But building a community doesn't stop at bringing familiar faces to the court. As you spend more time playing, you'll naturally meet other enthusiasts. Organizing pickleball events, like a casual weekend game day or a themed pickleball picnic, can be a great way to bond with fellow players. It's about both the love of the game and the joy of companionship, and you will be amazed at how many like-minded people are out there just waiting for you to find them.

Coach Chris Tip: A great way to meet new people and generate money for a cause is to organize a **pickleball fundraiser**. These are the perfect fundraising event format because of the wide range of people who can participate, which ranges from teens to seniors and all those in between!

36

Tournaments and Competitive Play

For those who've mastered the basics and are itching for a challenge, tournaments await. These events range from local gatherings organized by community centers to state or even national tournaments drawing players from far and wide.

Starting with local tournaments is a smart choice if you're new to the competitive scene. They provide a taste of the thrill without being too intimidating. But if you're aiming higher, then state and national tournaments might be your goal. These grand events often feature top-tier players, making them both a challenge to participate in and a spectacle to watch.

However, diving into the competitive scene requires preparation. Regular practice sessions, honing strategies, and hiring a coach can make a world of difference in your performance.

In the end, whether you're playing for the sheer joy of the game or the thrill of competition, pickleball is about community. It's not just a sport; it's a way of connecting with others, building friendships, and fostering a sense of belonging. So why wait? Grab a paddle and become part of the vibrant pickleball tournaments community!

Coach Chris Tip: Make sure you research and register for tournaments well in advance, because as the sport has grown, so has the interest and participation in tournaments. They fill up fast, but the memories will last a lifetime!

XII

Drills and Practice Routines

In this chapter, we will explore some amazing drills and routines to make you a pickleball overachiever. Whether you're practicing alone or with friends, these drills will help you take your game to the next level.

37

Drills for Improving Specific Skills

- **The Serve Accuracy Drill:** This is all about precision. Place cones or targets in different sections of the opponent's court. Now, challenge yourself. Try to hit each cone with your serve. Make it fun. Ask yourself, can you hit the cone 5 times in a row? The more you practice, the closer you get to being a serving champion.
- **The Volley Volley Drill:** Here's where things get quick! Stand close to the net with a partner. Your partner will hit volleys to you, and in return, you volley them back. It's a fast-paced drill, and it's all about reaction time. Keep a tally: how long can you both keep the volley going without the ball touching the ground?
- **Dink to Drop Shot**: Line up at the no volley zone opposite your partner. Play it "skinny," using only half of the court width. One player feeds balls cooperatively to the second player, with the second player gradually moving back to mid-court and then the baseline. After that, the second player begins transitioning back to the no volley zone, while

trying to keep shots low and just over the net. If a ball is left up, then player one should attack it. Keep score and exchange roles as the feeder.
- **Dink Battle:** The dink shot might seem simple, but it's a game-changer. For this, both players should stand near the net. The aim is to hit soft shots to each other that just clear the net. As the rally continues, you'll see how mastering this soft shot can be a strategic game-changer. Start by hitting cooperatively for four dinks, then work to keep your ball unattackable until your opponent makes an error and you strike for the win!

Coach Chris Tip: If you want to improve you have got to drill! Make drilling fun by recruiting a practice partner who is willing to challenge you, and then set up a standing day and time to hit in a place where you aren't tempted to play a game with the next two people that show up!

38

Structuring a Productive Practice Session

Every practice session should have a rhythm to it. Begin by doing some stretches and when ready, you and your partner can start hitting some soft dinks. Then, get things going by spending a few minutes rallying the ball back and forth with a partner.

Next, dedicate 20 minutes to a Skill Drill. Choose a specific drill, like the Serve Accuracy or Dink Battle drills. Track your progress and try to get better each time.

Next, engage in a Game Scenario for about 15 minutes. This is where you play a short game or simulate game situations with a partner. It's the cool part where you get to apply what you've practiced!

Finally, never forget the Cool Down. Spend 5 minutes slowing down. You could jog or walk around the court, engage in a relaxing stretch, and remember, always drink plenty of water.

Relaxing your muscles after rigorous practice is crucial.

Coach Chris Tip: If you want to improve your game, you've got to practice. No amount of game time can replace the benefits of drilling and working on skills development.

39

Solo Drills

Don't have a partner? It's okay; solo drills can be just as effective.

The Wall Rebound is perfect for those who want to improve hand-eye coordination and reaction time. All you need is a sturdy wall. Simply hit the ball against it and let it rebound back. Vary the pace and your shot selection, and consider buying a wall target so that you can clearly see your accuracy. It's simple but effective.

Next, you can focus on your serve with Serve Practice. Mark your target zones using chalk or cones. Try to ace your serves into these zones, and vary the pace, height, and depth to keep the returner guessing. The repetition will enhance your serving skills over time.

Finally, indulge in some Shadow Play. Visualize different game scenarios, move around, and practice your footwork, swings, and stances. You may not have a real opponent, but your imaginary one can give you quite the workout!

Coach Chris Tip: The best players practice individually and with partners. Don't let the lack of an available partner keep you from improving your game!

XIII

Advancing Your Game

Pickleball is more than just a game; it's a journey. And as with all journeys, there's always something new to explore and learn. Regardless of how long you've played, there's a path forward to enhance your skills. Now let's uncover the steps to elevate your game!

40

Seeking Coaching and Instruction

The best players in the world, no matter the sport, often have something in common: they've been guided by a coach or instructor. So, why is coaching so beneficial?

A coach provides personalized attention. They see you—not just as a player, but as an individual with unique strengths and areas to develop. Through their experienced eyes, they can pinpoint what you're doing right and where you could use a bit more practice.

Moreover, a coach introduces you to structured practice. Drills, exercises, strategies—you name it. These activities, often honed through years of experience, are designed to boost your agility, strength, and in-game intelligence.

Beyond techniques and drills, a coach offers something intangible: motivation. Their belief in your potential can often push you to new heights, inspiring you to challenge yourself every time you step onto the court.

Coach Chris Tip: I am continually amazed at how many former students send back notes to acknowledge how even small adjustments to their game helped them become better players. Endeavor to find some level of coaching, either through private training or via a clinic or drill. You may be surprised at the difference it can make in your game!

41

Advanced Strategies and Techniques

In this chapter, we'll dive into strategies and techniques to help you take your pickleball game to the next level.

Perfecting Your Serve

While the serve in pickleball isn't as aggressive as in tennis, it's still an essential tool to control the game from the outset.

- **Depth**: Aim for a deep serve, which forces your opponent to the back of the court. This limits their return options.
- **Placement**: Instead of just serving to the center, try serving wide to pull your opponent out of position.
- **Spin**: Introducing spin to your serve can make it unpredictable. Experiment with topspin and slice serves.

The Third Shot Drop

The third shot drop is a foundational shot for advanced play, allowing a team to transition from the baseline to the net.

- **Arc & Placement**: This shot should have a gentle arc, dropping it into the no volley zone (kitchen), making it difficult for opponents to hit it aggressively.
- **Consistency**: Practice until you can reliably get your third shot drop into the kitchen under pressure.

Improving Court Movement

Positioning is vital in pickleball.

- **Stay Low and Ready**: Adopt a slightly crouched stance, with your paddle up and ready.
- **Sidestep**: Instead of turning and running, sidestep (shuffle) to maintain readiness and balance.
- **Anticipation**: Read your opponents' body language to anticipate their next move.

Net Play & The Soft Game

Mastering soft play at the net can dramatically shift the momentum in your favor.

- **Dinking**: Engage in dink rallies to wait for an opportunity where you or your partner can put away a winning shot.
- **Blocks and Resets**: If an opponent hits a hard shot at you while you're at the net, focus on a controlled block or reset rather than a hard counterattack.

Effective Communication in Doubles

Doubles play requires impeccable teamwork.

- **Call Shots**: Always communicate with your partner about who will take the ball, especially in the middle.
- **Strategize Between Points**: Discuss strengths, weaknesses, and adapt strategies between points.

Analyzing Your Game

After playing, review and analyze your performance.

- **Record Your Matches**: Watching replays helps pinpoint strengths and weaknesses.
- **Seek Feedback**: Ask seasoned players or coaches for constructive feedback.

Physical Fitness

Pickleball, especially at advanced levels, can be taxing on the body.

- **Endurance Training**: Incorporate cardiovascular exercises to improve your stamina.
- **Strength Training**: Focus on leg strength for better movement and core strength for powerful shots.
- **Flexibility**: Regular stretching can prevent injuries and improve your reach on the court.

Mental Fortitude

Developing a strong mental game is as crucial as physical skills.

- **Stay Calm**: Deep breathing techniques can help maintain

calm during tense moments.
- **Visualize Success**: Positive visualization reinforces good habits and boosts confidence.

Coach Chris Tip: When you are able to pull all of these together, the next step is to practice, practice, practice!

42

Continuing Education and Staying Updated on Rule Changes

The world of pickleball is dynamic. It evolves. New rules emerge; old ones are revised. Staying current is not just a matter of compliance—it's about gaining an edge.

You could dedicate some time to reading the official pickleball rulebook. As tedious as it might seem, knowing the intricacies of the rules can give you an advantage on the court.

Consider attending classes or workshops. Many local community centers or sports clubs offer them, as does USA Pickleball and other organizations. They provide a dual benefit: you learn the latest rules and techniques while also connecting with fellow enthusiasts.

Lastly, the digital age is a blessing. Websites, forums, videos—there's a plethora of online resources dedicated to pickleball. Explore them. They're a treasure trove of strategies, updates, and insights.

***Coach Chris Tip*:** Never stop learning!

XIV

The Future of Pickleball

There is no question that pickleball is growing ever more popular. The paddles have evolved from wooden ones to advanced materials like graphite. The nets have become sturdier, and the balls have changed too. And as the equipment gets better, the strategies and skills in the game grow as well. Today, pickleball is not just a backyard game; It has transformed into a respected sport with worldwide appeal and championships.

43

Evolution of the Sport

The journey of pickleball from a local game to an international sensation has been nothing short of incredible. Across towns and cities, pickleball courts are popping up everywhere. Whether in schools, local parks, or exclusive sports clubs, these courts became a testament to the game's growing popularity.

And it hasn't been just about casual matches. Pickleball has begun to witness the rise of national and international tournaments. Enthusiasts from various corners of the world now travel long distances, either to participate or to be a spectator, or to cheer for their favorite players.

Not surprisingly, the collegiate level has begun to embrace pickleball. Over 125 colleges currently offer pickleball programs on their campuses. Following this development, the US Collegiate Championships have been established and will be held annually in January in Indianapolis, Indiana. They will be organized by the APP, the Association of Pickleball Professionals.

One of the unique features of pickleball has always been its universal appeal. It's not confined to a specific age group. Children, adults, and seniors all find camaraderie and competition in the sport. Based on its current trajectory, experts predict that in a few years, pickleball could stand shoulder to shoulder with sports like tennis or basketball. And there's always the Olympics!

44

How to be an Ambassador for the Game

If you've been bitten by the pickleball bug and are passionate about it, why not channel that energy to promote the game? By becoming an ambassador, you can introduce more people to the joys of pickleball.

Start by sharing your knowledge. When friends or family express curiosity about the game, take them to a court. Organize small friendly matches in your community or a mini-tournament. The key is to keep the atmosphere light and fun.

It's also essential to remain updated about the sport. Regularly brush up on the rules, familiarize yourself with its history, and stay in the loop with any recent developments or changes.

As an ambassador, it's crucial to promote not just the game but the spirit behind it. Respect for fellow players, adherence to rules, and displaying good sportsmanship should be at the forefront of your advocacy.

Consider becoming part of a larger community. Many places have pickleball clubs that regularly organize events, workshops, and matches. By joining, you can connect with fellow enthusiasts and collaborate on promotional activities.

And in this digital age, don't forget the power of social media. Platforms like Instagram, TikTok, and Facebook can be instrumental in showcasing your love for pickleball. Share videos of exciting rallies, offer tips for beginners, or narrate personal experiences that highlight the essence of the game.

Coach Chris Tip: I realized very quickly that pickleball was the best sport that I have ever played. The combination of a great workout, strategic problem solving, and players of all ages and abilities convinced me that I needed to do more than just play the sport, I needed to *learn* the sport and the culture surrounding it. I encourage everyone to go out, play, and then share your newfound hobby with those around you!

XV

Reasons to Love the Game

*The book started with 50 fun facts about the game, so let's end it with **100 reasons** to love the game!*

45

100 Reasons People Really Like Pickleball

1. Social interaction with friends and peers.
2. It's a fun and engaging form of exercise.
3. Provides a low-impact workout, reducing stress on joints.
4. Helps to improve cardiovascular health.
5. Enhances hand-eye coordination.
6. Develops agility and quick reflexes.
7. Burns calories and aids in weight management.
8. Builds muscle strength and endurance.
9. Offers a variety of skill levels, suitable for beginners to advanced players.
10. Can be played both indoors and outdoors, offering versatility.
11. Provides an opportunity to compete and enjoy friendly competition.
12. Increases flexibility and range of motion.
13. Boosts mental focus and concentration.
14. Helps to improve balance and stability.

15. Acts as a stress-reliever and mood enhancer.
16. Encourages teamwork and communication.
17. Builds camaraderie among players.
18. Offers a sense of achievement and progress in skill development.
19. Great way to make new friends and expand social circles.
20. Suitable for all ages, making it a family-friendly activity.
21. A fun way to stay active in retirement.
22. Helps to improve hand and arm strength.
23. Provides a break from daily routines and responsibilities.
24. Boosts self-esteem and self-confidence.
25. Creates a sense of belonging within a pickleball community.
26. Provides an opportunity to learn from experienced players.
27. Easy to learn, even for those with limited sports experience.
28. Inexpensive compared to other sports, with minimal equipment required.
29. Can be played in a recreational setting or in organized leagues.
30. Offers a variety of playing styles and strategies.
31. Great way to challenge yourself and set personal goals.
32. Allows players to adapt and modify gameplay based on their abilities.
33. Provides an opportunity to learn sportsmanship and fair play.
34. Encourages creativity and innovation in gameplay.
35. Improves hand dexterity and fine motor skills.
36. Promotes an active lifestyle and overall well-being.
37. Opportunity to attend pickleball events and tournaments.
38. Easy to find pickleball courts in various locations.

39. Helps to improve reaction times and decision-making skills.
40. A sport that can be played year-round, regardless of weather conditions.
41. Enhances mental acuity and problem-solving abilities.
42. Provides an enjoyable way to stay connected with loved ones.
43. Helps to improve patience and perseverance.
44. Creates lasting memories and shared experiences.
45. Encourages healthy competition and sportsmanship.
46. Offers an inclusive environment where players of all abilities are welcome.
47. Opportunities to travel and participate in pickleball vacations or retreats.
48. A non-intimidating sport for beginners, making it easy to get started.
49. Opportunity to compete in local, regional, and national tournaments.
50. Helps to relieve tension and release endorphins.
51. Fosters a sense of community and belonging.
52. Can be a gateway to other sports and physical activities.
53. Encourages a sense of adventure and exploration.
54. Builds resilience and the ability to bounce back from setbacks.
55. Provides an escape from daily stressors and worries.
56. Offers an outlet for creative expression during gameplay.
57. Provides an opportunity to learn and appreciate teamwork.
58. Opportunity to participate in charitable pickleball events and fundraisers.
59. A chance to challenge yourself physically and mentally.
60. Helps to improve hand-eye coordination and motor skills.

61. Can be played as a casual social activity or in a more competitive setting.
62. Provides an opportunity to learn and improve from constructive feedback.
63. Encourages continuous learning and skill improvement.
64. A sport that allows for spontaneous play and pickup games.
65. Provides a sense of accomplishment when mastering new shots and techniques.
66. Great way to bond with family members and friends.
67. Opportunity to try different paddle and ball combinations for personal preference.
68. Offers a welcoming and supportive community for new players.
69. A sport that can be enjoyed at any age, from young adults to seniors.
70. Allows for individual expression in playing style and strategy.
71. Provides an opportunity to be physically active without excessive strain.
72. Encourages a balanced and healthy lifestyle.
73. A sport that can be played for leisure or as a competitive pursuit.
74. Opportunity to volunteer and contribute to the pickleball community.
75. Offers a chance to challenge yourself against players of varying skill levels.
76. A sport that can be played in singles, doubles, or mixed doubles formats.
77. Provides an avenue for friendly banter and good-natured rivalry on the court.
78. Encourages respect for opponents and fellow players.

79. A sport that can be adapted to accommodate physical limitations or injuries.
80. Opportunity to participate in local pickleball meetups and groups.
81. Provides a sense of accomplishment when achieving personal goals.
82. Encourages regular physical activity and exercise routines.
83. A sport that can be played casually or with more competitive intensity.
84. Opportunity to engage in continuous improvement and self-development.
85. Provides a sense of purpose and motivation to stay active.
86. Encourages strategic thinking and tactical gameplay.
87. A sport that can be played in diverse settings, from community centers to parks.
88. Opportunity to learn and appreciate the rules and etiquette of the game.
89. Provides a sense of fulfillment when contributing to a winning team.
90. A sport that promotes inclusivity and diversity among players.
91. Opportunity to connect with pickleball enthusiasts from around the world.
92. Encourages setting and achieving both short-term and long-term goals.
93. Provides an opportunity to learn from experienced pickleball coaches.
94. A sport that offers a balance of individual skill and teamwork dynamics.
95. Opportunity to participate in pickleball-themed social events and parties.

96. Encourages a sense of playfulness and enjoyment during matches.
97. Provides a sense of community and support during gameplay.
98. A sport that can be played competitively in various age divisions.
99. Opportunity to represent and compete for local pickleball clubs or teams.
100. Provides a sense of belonging and camaraderie with fellow players.

46

Conclusion

Pickleball In No Time is the first in a series of books that will give you the background and knowledge to know the inner workings of the sport and become a better player. Now that we've explored its roots, the gear you need, the rules of play, and where this sport is headed, let's take a moment to wrap it all up.

Pickleball didn't start as a big sport like basketball or soccer. It began with just a few families looking to have fun. When it was invented back in 1965 by a group of his friends on Bainbridge Island, near Seattle, they had no idea that it would become the fastest growing sport in America, and among the fastest growing sports in the world.

What I love most about Pickleball is the simplicity of game, and how welcoming it is to players of all ages and skill levels. Its two most basic rules, no taking the ball out of the air in the no volley zone (kitchen) and that you must let the return of serve bounce, level out the playing field so that grandchildren can play with grandparents, and all groups in between. These rules keep the game exciting and give everyone a chance to play and win.

So, what's next for pickleball? The sky's the limit as more people find out how easy and enjoyable it is, further explaining why pickleball is so quickly growing in popularity. Schools are starting to include it in their physical education programs, celebrities are getting on board, and tournaments are becoming more frequent and competitive. There's a rapid global expansion and diligent work in progress to get the sport into the Olympics by 2032.

Hope to see you on the courts!

If you enjoyed the book, **please leave a review where you purchased it.**

Scan the QR code below to get added to our newsletter.

CONCLUSION

Pickleball In No Time

About the Author

Meet Coach Chris – a sports enthusiast, accomplished athlete, and passionate pickleball coach. With a background in racket sports and executive leadership, combined with his teaching experience at the Northbrook, IL, Park District, YMCAs of Metropolitan Chicago, and numerous camps and clinics with organizations such as Ken Herrmann Pickleball, Chris brings a unique blend of skills to his coaching. From tennis to racquetball to snow skiing, his love for physical and mental challenges has always been a driving force in his life. As a dedicated coach, he's committed to not only teaching pickleball but also nurturing leadership qualities, teamwork, and personal growth. Coach Chris's journey led him to write "PICKLEBALL IN NO TIME," a comprehensive guide that's packed with practical tips, clear instructions, and valuable insights. Whether you're a newcomer or an enthusiast, this book is your gateway to the exciting world of pickleball. Join Coach Chris on a journey of sports, learning, and exciting play.

You can connect with me on:
- https://www.pickleballinnotime.com

Subscribe to my newsletter:
- https://dink.zone

Made in the USA
Coppell, TX
19 August 2024

36183997R00105